Robert McCloskey's

HOMER PRICE

Student Guide

MEMORIA PRESS

www.MemoriaPress.com

Robert McCloskey's
HOMER PRICE

STUDENT GUIDE

Contributing Authors: Leigh Lowe, Brenda Janke, Brittany Mann, & Anne Parry

ISBN 978-1-61538-080-0

Cover Illustration: Starr Steinbach

Contents

Preparing to Read

Review

- Orally review any previous vocabulary.
- Review the plot of the book as read so far.
- Periodically review the concepts of character, setting, and plot.

Study Guide Preview

- **Reading Notes:** Read aloud together. This section gives key characters, places, terms that are relevant to a particular time period, etc.
- **Vocabulary:** Read aloud together so that students will recognize words when they come across them in their reading.
- **Comprehension Questions:** Read through these questions with students to encourage purposeful reading.

Reading

- Students read the chapter (or selection of the chapter for that lesson) independently or to the teacher (for younger students).
- For younger students, you can alternate between teacher-read and student-read passages. Model good reading skills. Encourage students to read expressively and smoothly. Teacher may occasionally take oral reading grades.
- While reading, mark each vocabulary word as you come across it.
- Have students take note in their study guide margins of pages where a comprehension question is answered.

After Reading

Vocabulary

- Look at each word within the context that it is used, and help students come up with the best synonym that defines the word. (Make sure it is a synonym students knows the meaning of.)
- Record the word's meaning in the students' study guides. (Use students' knowledge of Latin and other vocabulary to decipher meanings.)

Comprehension Questions

- Older students can answer these questions independently, but younger students (2nd-4th grade) need to answer the questions orally, form a good sentence, and then write it down, using correct punctuation, capitalization, and spelling. (You may want to write the sentence down for younger students after forming it orally, and then let students copy it perfectly.)
- It is not necessary to write the answer to every question. Some may be better answered orally.
- Answering questions and composing answers is a valuable learning activity. Questions require students to think; writing a concise answer is a good composition exercise.

Quotations and Discussion Questions

- Use the Quotations and Discussion Questions section of each lesson as a guide to your oral discussion of the key concepts in the chapter that may not be covered in the Comprehension Questions.
- These talking points can take your oral discussion to a higher level than covered in the students' written work. Use this time as an opportunity to introduce higher-level thinking. You can introduce concepts the students may not be mature enough to fully understand yet but that would be beneficial for them to begin thinking about.
- A key to the Discussion Questions is in the back of the Teacher Guide.

Enrichment

- The Enrichment activities include composition, copywork, dictation, research, mapping, drawing, poetry work, literary terms, and more.
- This section has a variety of activities in it, but the most valuable activity is composition. Your student should complete at least one composition assignment each week. Proof students' work and have students copy composition until grammatically perfect. Insist on clear, concise writing. For younger students, start with 2-3 sentences, and do the assignment together. The students can form good sentences orally as you write them down, and then the students copy them.
- These activities can be completed as time and interest allow. Do not feel you need to complete all of these activities. Choose the ones that you feel are the best use of your students' time.

Unit Review and Tests

- There is a unit review and a quiz or test following every few lessons (varies by individual guide).
- On the weeks that have these reviews and tests, you may want to do the review early in the week, and then drill it orally a couple of times before giving the test at the end of the week.
- A final comprehensive test is also included.
- Vocabulary Terms, Comprehension Questions, Discussion Questions, and Quiz Review questions with an asterisk in the Teacher Guide indicate important plot points that will appear on the quizzes and tests.

Reading Notes

ice box — a refrigerator; originally an insulated chest into which ice was placed to cool and preserve food

Musteline Mammal — a fur-bearing mammal, known for the foul-smelling, oily liquid they eject when frightened or in danger

Genus Mephitis — the Latin name for this family of mammals

Vocabulary

1. He decided to name the skunk **Aroma**.____________________
2. That's the last wire **soldered** and my new radio is finished. ____________________
3. The after shave lotion with the **distinctive** invigorating smell ____________________
4. The after shave lotion with the distinctive **invigorating** smell____________________
5. so he decided to sneak up and **investigate.**____________________
6. who had evidently gone to college and studied **zoology.** ____________________

Comprehension Questions

1. Where does Homer live? ____________________

2. What exciting news does Homer hear on his new radio? ____________________

3. Describe the suitcase used to hold the prize money and lotion. Why is this important to note?

4. Instead of being a happy celebration, the event becomes frightening. Why?

5. Why does Homer want to help N. W. Blott get his prize back?

Quotations

When Homer isn't going to school, or doing odd jobs, or playing with other boys, he works on his hobby which is building radios. He has a workshop in one corner of his room where he works in the evenings.

Discussion Questions

1. Using the quotation above, describe Homer. Give reasons for your answers.
2. Why is "Aroma" an appropriate name for Homer's pet skunk?
3. Briefly explain the classification system of the animal kingdom and the role Latin plays in it.

Enrichment

Focus Passage: Copy the fourth full paragraph on page 18 (beginning *"That, my dear friend …"*). Focus on correct spelling, punctuation, and capitalization.

Reading Notes

"I'll be switched."	an idiom meaning "I'm surprised!" or "I can't believe it!"
light button	a light switch
four dollars "in advance"	to pay a price before receiving an item or a service

Vocabulary

1. tried to **coax** Aroma out of the suitcase ______________________
2. Our present condition could be described as being a **trifle** overcrowded. ______________________
3. The robbers **gingerly** lifted the covers and peeked out ______________________
4. robbers aren't **accustomed** to going without shoes ______________________
5. the news **commentators** on the radio told about it too. ______________________

Comprehension Questions

1. Why do the robbers decide not to shoot Aroma in their hideout in the woods?

   ____

2. How does Homer figure out that the four guests at the tourist camp are the robbers?

   ____

   ____

3. Why does the sheriff wait to arrest the robbers at the tourist camp? ______________________

   ____

4. What does the sheriff mean when he says, "the boys and me can walk right in and snap the bracelets on 'em"? ______________________

5. Describe Homer's plan to catch the robbers. Who else plays an important part in this plan?

   ____

   ____

   ____

   ____

   ____

Quotations

While they were arguing Homer thought very hard. He guessed that something had better be done pretty quick or the robbers might decide to go before the sheriff got his hair cut. He thought of a plan, and without making a sound, he slipped away from the window and hurried to Aroma's hole under the house.

Discussion Questions

1. Find on page 20, "the air was filled with Aroma!" What is the double meaning of this phrase?
2. Do you agree with Homer's decision not to tell his mother about Aroma? Why or why not?
3. Note the picture of the robbers in bed on p. 25. Do you see anything amiss?

Enrichment

Noticing Details: Look for the answers to the following questions in Chapter 1 of *Homer Price*.

1. What kind of business does Homer's father own? ______________________________
2. What is Homer's hobby? ______________________________
3. What is Homer's cat's name? ______________________________
4. Where does Aroma live? ______________________________
____
5. How does Homer tame Aroma? ______________________________
____
6. What is the name of the person who won the slogan contest? ______________________________
7. How many guns does Homer think the robbers had in their room? ______________________________
____
8. Why do the robbers decide to all sleep in the same bed? ______________________________
____
____
9. To what country do the robbers plan to drive? ______________________________
____
10. What was Homer's reward for catching the robbers? ______________________________
____

Reading Notes

pitch horse shoes a game in which players toss horse shoes at a stake

mail-order house a catalogue company

Vocabulary

1. where the **villain** had put him ______
2. [He changes clothes like that] because he is so **modest**. ______
3. the villain, who turned out to be a very **notorious** criminal. ______
4. with **chromium** trimmings ______
5. the Super-Duper's **monogram** on the side. ______

Comprehension Questions

1. Why is Homer less impressed with the Super-Duper comics than Freddy? ______
2. How does Homer explain the incredible feats of the hero in the movies? ______
3. Who are Freddy and Louis, and why are they heading into town? ______
4. Describe the Super-Duper's car. ______
5. What is the name of the movie the boys see? What happens in the film? ______

Quotations

"Yeh, but it's only a story," said Homer. "And the story's always the same. The Super-Duper always hits things and breaks them up, and a villain always tries to bomb him, or shoot him with a cannon or a gun or an electric ray. Then he always rescues the pretty girl and gets the villain in the end."

Discussion Questions

1. What is the Super-Duper's reason for not flying or bending horse shoes? Do you think that is the real reason? Why not?
2. Does the Super-Duper remind you of a well-known comic hero? Who is it? Give evidence from the story of the similarities between Super-Duper and this hero.

Enrichment

Focus Passage: Copy the conversation between Homer and Freddy beginning on page 37. (Begin with *"Gosh, Freddy ..."* and end on the next page with "Let's go pitch horse shoes.")

Remember to begin a new paragraph with each new quotation. Focus on correct spelling, punctuation, and capitalization.

Reading Notes

barbed-wire fence	twisted strands of fence wire with sharp barbs at regular intervals
iodine	a liquid used as an antiseptic for wounds

Vocabulary

1. "Golly," said Freddy in a **quavery** voice ______
2. Homer tried hard to make it sound **convincing**. ______
3. and then, the **incredible** happened. ______
4. that same Super-Duper who **defied** the elements ______
5. He made faces, just like anybody else, when it was **daubed** on. ______

Comprehension Questions

1. What happens to the Super-Duper as he leaves the cinema? ______
2. How do Freddy and Louis expect the Super-Duper to get himself out of trouble? ______
3. How did the Super-Duper end up in the ditch? ______
4. How do the boys help the Super-Duper? ______
5. What surprises the boys most about the scene? ______

Quotations

The Super-Duper didn't lift the car, no, not yet. He looked at the dent that a fence post had made in his shiny red fender, and then, *the incredible happened. That colossal-osal, gigantic-antic, Super-Duper, that same Super-Duper who defied the elements, who was so strong that he broke up battleships like toothpicks, who was so tough that cannon-balls bounced off his chest, yes, who was* tougher *than steel, he stooped down and said … "Ouch!"*

Discussion Question

As the boys first see the car in the ditch from a distance, do you think Homer is completely convinced that the Super-Duper was not hit by an electric ray? Find the words in the story that support your answer.

Enrichment

Create your own comic strip: Think of four short sentences that summarize the entire sequence of events in Chapter 2, and write them on the lines below. Use the words "first," "next," "then," and "finally" to help you.

Then, find the comic strip illustration page in the Appendix and draw a picture to go with each of the sentences you wrote. Use as much detail as possible in your illustrations.

1. First, ____________________

2. Next, ____________________

3. Then, ____________________

4. Finally, ____________________

Reading Notes

Red Cross	an international organization that cares for the wounded and sick in wartime and following natural disasters
receipt	an old word for a recipe
pinochle	a type of card game
tarnation	an expression used to show anger or annoyance

Vocabulary

1. a weakness for labor saving **devices**. ______
2. Sometimes she became **unkindly disposed** toward him ______
3. Uncle Ulysses just **frittered away** his spare time ______
4. a **chauffeur** helped a lady out of the rear door ______
5. it rolled neatly down a little **chute** ______

Comprehension Questions

1. Describe Uncle Ulysses. ______

2. Mr. Gabby describes himself as "a sandwich man." In what way is he like a sandwich?

3. In addition to Mr. Gabby, who else visits the lunch room? Describe her. ______

4. What concerns Homer about making the doughnuts with Mr. Gabby and the lady?

5. How does the task go wrong? How many doughnuts does Mr. Gabby count?

Quotations

Homer pushed the button marked "Stop" and there was a little click, but nothing happened. The rings of batter kept right on dropping into the hot fat, and an automatic gadget kept right on turning them over, and another automatic gadget kept right on giving them a little push and the doughnuts kept right on rolling down the little chute, all ready to eat.

Discussion Questions

1. Reread the quotation above. Where else do you notice these words in the story? Why do you think the author repeats them so many times?
2. Uncle Ulysses is a huge fan of labor-saving devices. List some common labor-saving devices we use today. Choose one that you think is the most helpful, and support your choice by explaining how this device makes your life easier.
3. The author of this book likes to have fun choosing the names of his characters. Note the names of Homer's aunt and uncle. Why are they interesting? How does Mr. Gabby's name fit his personality?

Enrichment

Focus passage: Copy the complete first paragraph on page 59 (beginning with *"'Yes,' said Homer."*).

Be careful not to lose your place as you copy all the repeating words. Focus on correct spelling, punctuation, and capitalization.

Reading Notes

create the market these are all business terms having to do with buying and selling items
supply and demand
merchandising

Vocabulary

1. the lunch room was a **calamity** of doughnuts! ______
2. You got the doughnuts, ya gotta **create the market**. ______
3. It's **balancing the demand with the supply**. ______
4. the sheriff cast a **suspicious** eye on Mr. Gabby ______
5. Neatest trick of **merchandising** I ever seen. ______
6. Aunt Aggy was looking **sceptical*** ______

*NOTE: Standard U.S. spelling is *skeptical*.

Comprehension Questions

1. As the doughnut crisis grows, what are Uncle Ulysses' concerns? ______

2. What does Mr. Gabby suggest to help sell all the extra doughnuts? ______

3. What happens during the doughnut crisis that adds to the day's worries? ______

4. Why do people begin helping to solve the problem? ______________________________

____

____

5. Who finds the missing bracelet? ______________________________

Quotations

Before twenty more doughnuts could roll down the little chute he shouted, "SAY! I know where the bracelet is! It was lying here on the counter and got mixed up in the batter by mistake! The bracelet is cooked inside one of these doughnuts!"

Who said this? ______________________

Discussion Questions

1. How does Homer provide both the cause and the solution to the doughnut problem?

2. Think of a worthwhile item for which you would like to create a market (i.e., cause people to desire it more). Discuss ways in which you could do this.

3. What does Uncle Ulysses say right after he walks into the lunch room and sees the doughnut mess? How does his response add humor to the story? What is that kind of humor called?

Enrichment

Quotation Review: How good is your memory? Supply the name of the speaker for each quotation below. Quotations are taken from Chapters 1-3.

______________________ 1. *"That, my dear friend, is* not *a thing. It is a Musteline Mammal."*

______________________ 2. *"Yep! that was sure one smell job of swelling."*

______________________ 3. *"I'm sorry, boys, but I haven't time today."*

______________________ 4. *"I haven't had so much fun in years. I* really *haven't!"*

______________________ 5. *"My, how that boy does grow!"*

______________________ 6. *"Yeh, but it's only a story. And the story's always the same."*

______________________ 7. *"I GAWT IT!!"*

______________________ 8. *"He's an awful modest fellow."*

______________________ 9. *"Well, I'll be dunked!!"*

______________________ 10. *"A traveling man in outdoor advertising. I'm a sandwich man."*

Character: ***Who** is in the story*

1. Who is the main character in this book? How would you describe him?

____

____

____

2. List five other characters from Chapters 1-3. ____

____

____

____

Setting: ***Time** and **place** in which the story happens*

1. What is the setting of *Homer Price*? ____

____

____

2. List some ways in which life in the story is different from your own. ____

____

____

____

____

Plot: ***Action** or **what happens** in the story*

Sequence the following events from Chapter 1 in the order in which they happened.

_________ Homer and Aroma find the hideout of the robbers, and Aroma adds his scent to the money.

_________ Homer gathers the robbers' clothes and guns, and marches them to the sheriff.

_________ When the robbers rent a cabin, Homer recognizes them and reports them to the sheriff.

_________ Homer finds and tames a skunk, named Aroma, to be his pet.

_________ Aroma is sent into the cabin and frightens the robbers into staying awhile.

_________ The award money and lotion from Mr. Dreggs' advertising contest are stolen by four robbers.

Character Identification

Write the name of the character on the line next to the description.

1. ____________________ is convinced the Super-Duper is a very modest fellow
2. ____________________ a traveling salesman, a "sandwich" man
3. ____________________ has a weakness for labor-saving devices
4. ____________________ wrecked his car when he dodged a skunk
5. ____________________ own and run a tourist camp and service station
6. ____________________ has a chauffeur named Charles
7. ____________________ impressed with how fast Homer is growing
8. ____________________ solves problems using common sense
9. ____________________ Homer's pet skunk
10. ____________________ often mixes up his words

Illustration

Illustrate Homer Price in your favorite setting from Chapters 1-3.

Quiz I Review

VOCABULARY: Write the letter of the vocabulary word on the line next to its definition.

_______ 1. machines
_______ 2. famously bad
_______ 3. criminal
_______ 4. distrustful
_______ 5. one-of-a-kind
_______ 6. tempt
_______ 7. disaster
_______ 8. used to; familar with
_______ 9. challenged
_______ 10. wavering; shaky
_______ 11. cross; aggravated
_______ 12. carefully
_______ 13. doubtful
_______ 14. scent
_______ 15. symbol; initials
_______ 16. slide
_______ 17. a tiny bit
_______ 18. the study of animal life
_______ 19. wasted
_______ 20. spread; smeared

A. distinctive
B. accustomed
C. notorious
D. quavery
E. devices
F. calamity
G. suspicious
H. defied
I. coax
J. villain
K. aroma
L. zoology
M. gingerly
N. monogram
O. daubed
P. chute
Q. unkindly disposed
R. frittered away
S. sceptical
T. trifle

SHORT ANSWER: Answer the following questions in complete sentences.

1. Describe Homer Price, the main character of this story. ______________________________

____

____

____

2. What is Homer's opinion about comics in general, and the Super-Duper?

____

____

____

3. How does Homer's common sense help him solve the mystery of the missing bracelet?

____

____

____

QUOTATION IDENTIFICATION: Write the name of the speaker on the line next to each quotation.

1. ______________________ "Just *wait* till you taste these doughnuts!"
2. ______________________ "SAY! I know where the bracelet is!"
3. ______________________ "Naaw! Nothing can hurt the Super-Duper because he's too tough."
4. ______________________ "We will have to get rid of that animal right away ..."
5. ______________________ "Well, I'll be switched."
6. ______________________ "We must get rid of these doughnuts before Aggy gets here!"
7. ______________________ "A real radio broadcast from Centerburg! I'll have to see that!"
8. ______________________ "I didn't want to hit him and get this new car all smelled up."
9. ______________________ "I lost count at twelve hundred and two and that was quite a while back."
10. ______________________ "Our present condition could be described as being a trifle overcrowded."

Reading Notes

rheumatism a condition of the joints and muscles that causes bodily aches and pains
drive a hard bargain to require tough conditions before coming to an agreement with a person
clinch the bargain refers to an action that brings final, solid agreement between two people

Vocabulary

1. Miss Terwilliger is … an **accomplished** knitter ______________________
2. he would make an **ideal** husband for some fine woman ______________________
3. provide the **diversion** that the trotting races have ______________________
4. I **appeal** to your sense of county pride. ______________________
5. Do not **spurn** the offer. ______________________
6. an assistant to help with the **maneuvering** of his ball of string. ______________________

Comprehension Questions

1. Describe Miss Terwilliger. What is unusual about her? ______________________

____

2. Why does Aunt Aggy think it would be difficult for a woman to put up with Uncle Telly?

____

3. What does Judge Shank suggest as an alternative to the races for the fair? ______________________

____

____

4. On what condition do Uncle Telly and the sheriff agree to Judge Shank's suggestion? ______________________

____

____

5. Describe the rules of the contest. ______________________

____

____

____

Quotations

Homer's Uncle Telly lived all by himself in a trim little house near the railroad. Homer's mother always said, "It's a shame that Uncle Telly had to live alone because he would make an ideal husband for some fine woman like Miss 'T'." Aunt Aggy would always answer, "But I don't know how any fine woman could put up with his carryings on!"

Discussion Questions

1. Burning leaves reminds Homer and the sheriff of other things that commonly occur in the fall. What are these fall events? Can you think of others not mentioned?
2. We've already seen that the author likes to have fun with the names of his characters. Can you name four characters found in Greek literature or Greek mythology from which the author has drawn names for the characters of this book? Discuss these characters briefly.

Enrichment

Focus Passage: Copy the last full paragraph on page 78 (beginning with *"Uhumpf! Prize or no prize …"*).

Be careful to copy all quotation marks accurately. Focus on correct spelling, punctuation, and capitalization.

Reading Notes

double cross to betray someone by violating a prior agreement

parasol a small, light umbrella carried as protection from the sun

watch like a hawk to watch someone very carefully (hawks are known for their good vision)

all's fair in love means there are no "rules" when one is trying to gain the love of another

Vocabulary

1. He was multiplying 3.1416 by the **diameter** ____________________
2. "Do you think," said the sheriff … winking **frantically** ____________________
3. the county fair will be an **unprecedented** success. ____________________
4. each **accused** the other of telling about the agreement. ____________________
5. the sheriff **trudged** up and congratulated Miss Terwilliger ____________________
6. I guess they're the **undisputed** champions now. ____________________

Comprehension Questions

1. Who is the new contestant in the contest? Why is this surprising? ____________________

   ____

2. What phrase is repeated three times at the beginning of the chapter and, again, four times at the end?

   ____

3. As the story reports the progress of Miss Terwilliger around the track, it also describes her clothing. Describe her blue dress at each point. ____________________

   ____

   ____

   ____

4. How do you think Miss Terwilliger won the contest? ____________________

   ____

5. Despite losing the String Saver contest, Uncle Telly wins big. Explain. ____________________

   ____

Quotations

Practically every woman who was there that day knew how the clever Miss Terwilliger had won the championship. They enjoyed it immensely and laughed among themselves, but they didn't give away the secret because they thought, "all's fair in love," and besides a woman ought to be allowed to make up her own mind.

Discussion Questions

1. When Miss Terwilliger says she wants to enter the contest, the judge says, "The American female is beginning to find her rightful place in the business and public life of this nation." He is said to have made a "fancy speech about 'woman's rights.'" To what are these sentences referring?
2. Where in the United States is Niagara Falls? For what is it known? Find it on a map.

Enrichment

Studying Context Clues: An author often provides written clues to prepare the reader for what will happen later in the story. One way to do this is to repeat lines or phrases he wants the reader to notice. A careful reader will look for these clues to gain deeper understanding and enjoyment of the story. Look for context clues in Chapter 4 of *Homer Price* by answering the questions below.

1. The best example of repetition is the phrase "robin's-egg blue." Where is it repeated, and how does this add to the story? ____________________

____

____

2. Find four places where we are told the same information about Miss Terwilliger. How does this offer a clue to her participation in the contest? ____________________

____

____

3. Which page reveals a clue that Uncle Telly will indeed marry Miss Terwilliger? ____________________

____

4. Besides what we know about Miss Terwilliger, we are given a clue about yarn that hints at how she wins the contest later on. Can you find it? ____________________
5. What phrase about men is repeated? How does it help explain the end of the story?

____

____

____

Reading Notes

blue plate special a main course of a restaurant meal, offered at a special price

gaiters a cloth or leather covering for the leg, from the instep to the ankle or knee

Rip Van Winkle a story character who sleeps 100 years, then returns from the hills to society

almanac an annual publication composed of lists, charts, and other general information

Vocabulary

1. conversation had already **dwindled** to nothing at all. ____________________
2. if I bring you a new customer I get a **commission**. ____________________
3. he might be a **fugitive** in disguise ____________________
4. or maybe one of these **amnesia** cases ____________________
5. how clever the sheriff was at **deducing** things. ____________________
6. not exactly, a **hermit** … first time he saw people for thirty years. ____________________

Comprehension Questions

1. Why are the men in the barber shop especially interested in the stranger that comes to town? ____________________
2. Why is the sheriff uneasy about the stranger? How does Homer help the sheriff? ____________________
3. What is the stranger's nickname? How does he get this name? ____________________
4. What does Homer learn about the stranger? ____________________
5. What makes Mr. Murphy's mouse trap so unique? ____________________

Quotations

It wasn't because this car was old, old enough to be an antique; or because some strange business was built onto it; or that the strange business was covered with a large canvas. No, that wasn't what made Homer and the sheriff, and Uncle Ulysses, and the barber stare so long. It was the car's driver.

Discussion Questions

1. After his first impressions, how does the sheriff describe the stranger? Why is this humorous?
2. Contrast the information people in the story use to "judge" others. What conclusion can you draw?
3. Homer says Mr. Murphy read that "if a man can make a better mouse trap than anybody else, the world will beat a path to his house." What does this mean? What is the double meaning here?

Enrichment

Focus Passage: Copy the last three paragraphs on page 105 (beginning with "Bright and early …" and ending with "… do the finding!").

Be careful to indent new paragraphs and to copy all quotation marks accurately.
Focus on correct spelling, punctuation, and capitalization.

Reading Notes

thing of a jig — a slang term for an unnamed, unknown object
license plate — a metal sign on a car, showing official permission to own and operate
Pied Piper of Hamelin — a story character who charms first mice, and then children, into following him

Vocabulary

1. **painstakingly** arranged the spiral ramps ____________________
2. *The **Pied** Piper of Hamelin* ____________________
3. Mr. Murphy was very **flustered** ____________________
4. The mice came out in a **torrent**. ____________________
5. That music has **pixied** these children! ____________________

Comprehension Questions

1. How does Homer's common sense prompt him to be suspicious of the pied piper?

____

____

2. How much is Mr. Murphy's fee for removing mice? Why isn't he allowed to keep the fee?

____

3. What does the librarian discover about the stranger? Why is she so upset by it?

____

____

4. How does the sheriff get Mr. Murphy to release the children? ____________________

____

____

5. How does Mr. Murphy misunderstand the sheriff, and what happens as a result?

____

____

6. In what way does Homer's cleverness protect the children from possible danger? ____________________

____

Quotations

There's no telling how this de-mousing would have ended if the children's librarian hadn't come rushing up shouting "Sheriff! Sheriff! Quick! We guessed the wrong book! ... *Yes!" gasped the children's librarian, "not* Rip Van Winkle, *but* another *book,* The Pied Piper of Hamelin!"

Discussion Questions

1. You have learned to be watching for context clues in a story that foretell coming events. Find a clue on page 113 that hints at coming trouble.

Enrichment

DRAWING COMPARISONS AND CONTRASTS:

Read the story *Rip Van Winkle* (found in the Appendix of this guide).
Compare and contrast this story with Chapter 5 of *Homer Price*, using the chart on the following page.

What is the moral of the story *Rip Van Winkle*? ______________________________

____

____

____

____

Read the story *The Pied Piper of Hamelin* (found in the Appendix of this guide).

Compare and contrast this story with Chapter 5 of *Homer Price*, using the chart on the following page.

What is the moral of the story *The Pied Piper of Hamelin*? ______________________________

____

____

____

Read the story of Odysseus (can be found in *Famous Men of Greece*, Memoria Press).

How is the ancient story of Odysseus similar to *Homer Price*, Chapter 5? ______________________________

____

____

____

Rip Van Winkle

List the ways in which Mr. Murphy is **similar** to Rip Van Winkle in this chapter.

List the ways in which Mr. Murphy is **different** from Rip Van Winkle in this chapter.

Illustrate your favorite portion of *Rip Van Winkle* below:

The Pied Piper of Hamelin

List the ways in which Mr. Murphy is **similar** to the Pied Piper in this chapter.

List the ways in which Mr. Murphy is **different** from the Pied Piper in this chapter.

Illustrate your favorite portion of *The Pied Piper of Hamelin* below:

Reading Notes

too many cooks spoil the soup	too many workers at the same job can get in each other's way
pet theories	favorite ideas or beliefs
landscape architect	someone who plans beautiful gardens around houses
era	a period of time characterized by particular circumstances

Vocabulary

1. Because it isn't **imperative** that I hafta go fishing. ______
2. help me adjust the timing **mechanism** in this toaster. ______
3. she has a **receptive** mind ______
4. they could be **replicas** of the Enders homestead ______
5. That's the **principle**! ______
6. and a touch of **ingenuity** ______

Comprehension Questions

1. Who is Miss Enders? How did she come to live in Centerburg? ______
2. Why does Uncle Ulysses think so highly of Miss Enders? ______
3. What plan does Miss Enders propose to help the housing shortage? ______
4. Why does this project excite Uncle Ulysses? ______
5. How does the project change, and what is the reasoning behind this change? ______

Quotations

"That's the principle that Henry Ford applied to making autos. Yep! Autos are mass produced, like doughnuts; ships are built like doughnuts; airplanes and refrigerators, and now houses. *Yessiree, the* modern *house ought to be mass produced—just like cars or ships or planes. Yessiree!"*

Who said this? ______________________ To whom is he speaking? ______________________

Discussion Questions

1. Who was Henry Ford and where did he live? For what is he famous? How does Uncle Ulysses explain the benefits of mass production and assembly lines?
2. At the end of this section of the chapter, Miss Enders says, "Just think. Last week there were only grass and trees and squirrels on this spot!" Do you think the author is suggesting that this is a good change or a bad one? What do you think?

Enrichment

Focus Passage: Copy the fifth full paragraph on page 129 (beginning with *"That's the principle ..."* and ending with *"Snap!"*).

Watch for the quotation marks and copy them accurately. Focus on correct spelling, punctuation, and capitalization.

Reading Notes

Whistler's Mother a famous painting by James McNeill Whistler

proud as Punch from the famous puppets Punch and Judy; Punch is proud of his wrong deeds

pantomime to act a part without using words

elixir a substance believed to maintain life indefinitely

Vocabulary

1. newspaper said in an **editorial** ________________
2. The union surely wouldn't **object** to that! ________________
3. Couldn't you **arbitrate** or something? ________________
4. the union will have to **picket** ________________
5. found forty-two pounds of **edible fungus** growing ________________
6. the Indian uprising was **quelled** ________________

Comprehension Questions

1. What is the argument between Uncle Ulysses and Dulcey Dooner? ________________

   ____

2. How do the new tenants find their way to their own homes? ________________

   ____

   ____

3. Who founded the city that is now Centerburg? What was the city's first name? ________________

   ____

4. Why were the street signs not erected after the pageant ended? ________________

   ____

   ____

5. How did the Dulcey Dooner incident benefit the city? ________________

   ____

   ____

Quotations

Another house, like all the others, stood in its place. One hundred and one houses, all alike, down to the last door knob! Each with its climbing rose bush, two dwarf cedars, and maple tree sodded round about. Just as alike as one hundred and one doughnuts, and nothing, no nothing to count from to find out which was which and whose was whose. There was a mad scramble, with much shouting, with the deserving tenants trying frantically to find out which house was which.

Discussion Questions

1. What items are included in each house in the new suburb? Is this good or bad? Why?
2. What is a "union"? What problem did the Street Sign Putter Uppers Union cause for Centerburg?

Character Identification

Write the name of the speaker on the line next to each quotation.

1. ______________________ *"But I don't know how any fine woman could put up with his carryings on!"*
2. ______________________ *"It's marvelous, simply marvelous!"*
3. ______________________ *"It's just to be on the safe side."*
4. ______________________ *"Isn't it* wonderful *that we have* so *much in common?"*
5. ______________________ *"Yessiree, the* modern *house ought to be mass produced."*
6. ______________________ *"Well, Sheriff,* I *judge everybody by their* feet, *and their* shoes.*"*
7. ______________________ *"Get 'em low! Get 'em go! Durnit, Let 'em go!"*
8. ______________________ *"Ya see … I make all the union rules, pay all the dues (and collect them too) so what I say goes."*
9. ______________________ *"Wind it tight; don't let anybody say that my string isn't wound right!"*
10. ______________________ *"Sheriff! Sheriff! Quick!* We guessed the wrong book!*"*

Character: *Who is in the story*

1. List the minor characters from Chapters 4-6. ____________________

2. Choose one of the minor characters above, and write a sentence about something they did that you thought was humorous. ____________________

Setting: *Time and place in which the story happens*

Chapters 4-6 are set in the fall season. Using your senses (sight, smell, hearing, taste, touch), write two sentences describing fall. ____________________

Plot: *Action or what happens in the story*

Sequence the following events from Chapter 5 in the order in which they happened.

_______ Mr. Murphy misunderstands the sheriff and releases all the mice back into the town.

_______ Mr. Murphy agrees to catch all the town mice and drive them out of town to release them.

_______ An unusual-looking stranger comes to Centerburg, causing the sheriff to be uneasy.

_______ All the town's children follow Mr. Murphy as he collects the mice in his amazing machine.

_______ The librarian tells the sheriff "Old Rip" is really more like the Pied Piper, and must be stopped.

_______ Homer learns that "Old Rip" has made a special mouse trap and brings him to the mayor.

Character Identification

Write the name of the character on the line next to the description.

1. ______________________ refuses to put up street signs unless he is paid $10 per sign
2. ______________________ judges people by their hair
3. ______________________ hires the stranger to catch all the town's mice
4. ______________________ donates some of her property to build a new suburb
5. ______________________ thinks Miss Terwilliger is a great cook and wants to marry her
6. ______________________ wants to cut expenses at the fair by holding a string-saver contest
7. ______________________ discovers important information by researching books at the library
8. ______________________ warns the sheriff that the children of Centerburg may be in danger
9. ______________________ a very clever woman
10. ______________________ very enthusiastic about mass production and assembly lines

Illustration

Illustrate Homer Price in your favorite setting from Chapters 4-6.

Quiz 2 Review

VOCABULARY: Write the letter of the vocabulary word on the line next to its definition.

_______ 1.	absolutely necessary	A. ideal
_______ 2.	one who lives alone	B. frantically
_______ 3.	stopped	C. unprecedented
_______ 4.	rapidly, with nervous activity	D. amnesia
_______ 5.	multi-colored	E. hermit
_______ 6.	copies, models	F. pixied
_______ 7.	never before seen	G. imperative
_______ 8.	put a magic spell on	H. replicas
_______ 9.	memory loss	I. quelled
_______ 10.	perfect	J. pied
_______ 11.	became gradually less	K. spurn
_______ 12.	changing movement or direction	L. maneuvering
_______ 13.	fee	M. accused
_______ 14.	agitated; confused	N. dwindled
_______ 15.	disapprove of	O. fugitive
_______ 16.	turn down; decline	P. commission
_______ 17.	escaped criminal	Q. torrent
_______ 18.	cleverness; inventiveness	R. flustered
_______ 19.	charged; blamed	S. ingenuity
_______ 20.	flood	T. object

SHORT ANSWER: Answer the following questions in complete sentences.

1. What did Miss Terwilliger do that displayed her cleverness?____________________

2. What very important difference is there between Mr. Murphy and the Pied Piper at the end of the chapter?

3. Describe one benefit and one harmful effect that occurred in Centerburg as a result of mass production.

QUOTATION IDENTIFICATION: Write the name of the speaker on the line in front of each quotation.

1. ____________________ "… not *Rip Van Winkle*, but *another* book, *The Pied Piper of Hamelin*!"
2. ____________________ "Nope, it's ten dollars or nothing."
3. ____________________ "That woman certainly can cook!"
4. ____________________ "I wondered where my jelly beans were disappearing to!"
5. ____________________ "I have a beautiful ball of yarn, all colors of the rainbow."
6. ____________________ "I appeal to your sense of county pride. Do not spurn the offer."
7. ____________________ "That's the principle!"
8. ____________________ "This is where Ezekiel buried it! And this is where the Homestead stood!"
9. ____________________ "I think I'll start savin' paper bags or bottle caps!"
10. ____________________ "I've decided … to build a few homes on the family property."

Vocabulary Crossword

Use your vocabulary knowledge from reading *Homer Price* to complete the following crossword:

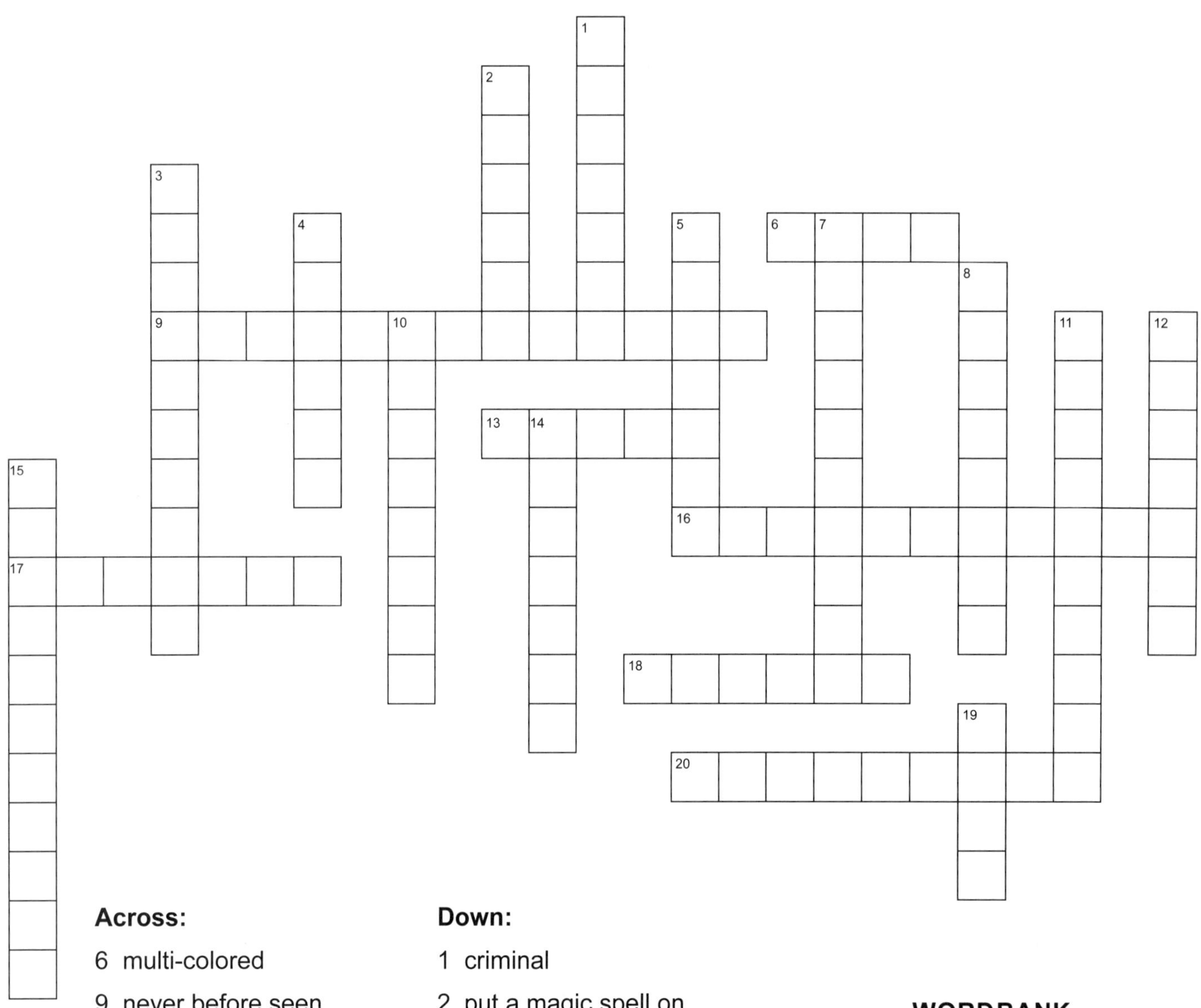

Across:

6 multi-colored
9 never before seen
13 perfect
16 one-of-a-kind
17 memory loss
18 challenged
20 famously bad

Down:

1 criminal
2 put a magic spell on
3 used to; familiar with
4 one who lives alone
5 stopped
7 absolutely necessary
8 copies; models
10 disaster
11 distrustful
12 wavering; shaky
14 machines
15 rapidly, w/ nervous activity
19 tempt

WORDBANK

distinctive	ideal
coax	frantically
accustomed	unprecedented
villain	amnesia
notorious	hermit
quavery	pied
defied	pixied
devices	imperative
calamity	replicas
suspicious	quelled

Character Identification

Using the following names, match each name to a description and write the name on the line.

Freddy	Miss Terwilliger	Aroma	the librarian	Homer
Mr. Gabby	the sheriff	Uncle Telly	Uncle Ulysses	Miss Enders

1. ______________________ solves problems using common sense

2. ______________________ Homer's pet skunk

3. ______________________ has a weakness for labor-saving devices

4. ______________________ donates some of her property to build a new suburb

5. ______________________ a traveling salesman, a "sandwich" man

6. ______________________ often mixes up his words

7. ______________________ warns the sheriff that the town's children are in danger

8. ______________________ is convinced the Super-Duper is a very modest fellow

9. ______________________ thinks Miss Terwilliger is a great cook

10. ______________________ a very clever woman

Who Said That?

Write the name of the speaker on the line in front of each quotation.

1. ______________________ "I wondered where my jelly beans were disappearing to!"

2. ______________________ "SAY! I know where the bracelet is!"

3. ______________________ "That, my dear friend, is *not* a thing. It is a Musteline Mammal."

4. ______________________ "He's an awful modest fellow."

5. ______________________ "Isn't it *wonderful* that we have *so* much in common?"

6. ______________________ "My, how that boy does grow!"

7. ______________________ "A traveling man in outdoor advertising. I'm a sandwich man."

8. ______________________ "Nope, it's ten dollars or nothing."

9. ______________________ "Well, I'll be dunked!!"

10. ______________________ "It's marvelous, simply marvelous!"

Ordering Events

Number the events of each chapter in the order in which they occurred.

Chapter 1

_________ When the robbers rent a cabin, Homer recognizes them and reports them to the sheriff.

_________ Homer gathers the robbers' clothes and guns, and marches them to the sheriff.

_________ The award money and lotion from Mr. Dreggs' advertising contest are stolen by four robbers.

_________ Aroma is sent into the cabin and frightens the robbers into staying awhile.

_________ Homer and Aroma find the hideout of the robbers, and Aroma adds his scent to the money.

_________ Homer finds and tames a skunk, named Aroma, to be his pet.

Chapter 2

_________ The Super-Duper wrecks his car trying to avoid a skunk crossing the road.

_________ Super-Duper gives the boys a gift of his comic books.

_________ The boys meet Super-Duper at the theater, where he refuses to fly for them.

_________ The boys pull the car out of the ditch and tow it to Homer's father's garage.

_________ Homer, Freddy, and Louis look at Super-Duper comic books, but Homer is not impressed.

_________ A fast car speeding around the curve passes the boys driving their horse and wagon.

Chapter 3

_________ The wealthy woman comes back looking for her lost bracelet.

_________ A friendly salesman comes to the lunch room for coffee and doughnuts.

_________ The doughnut machine breaks and won't stop producing doughnuts.

_________ Homer offers a reward for the bracelet and tells people it will be found in a doughnut.

_________ Homer and Mr. Gabby think of a way to sell all the extra doughnuts.

_________ A wealthy woman arrives at the lunch room and offers to make her special doughnut batter.

Chapter 4

_________ The sheriff and Uncle Telly agree to a String Saving contest at the county fair.

_________ Miss Terwilliger surprises everyone and enters the contest herself.

_________ Uncle Telly and Miss Terwilliger are married. The sheriff decides to save bottle caps.

_________ The men decide that Miss Terwilliger should be the secret “prize” for the contest.

_________ Miss Terwilliger wears her blue dress and wins the contest.

_________ We meet Miss Terwilliger and learn that both Uncle Telly and the sheriff want to marry her.

Chapter 5

_________ Homer learns that “Old Rip” has made a special mouse trap and brings him to the mayor.

_________ Mr. Murphy agrees to catch all the town mice and drive them out of town to release them.

_________ The librarian tells the sheriff “Old Rip” is really more like the Pied Piper, and must be stopped.

_________ All the town’s children follow Mr. Murphy as he collects the mice in his amazing machine.

_________ Mr. Murphy misunderstands the sheriff and releases all the mice back into the town.

_________ An unusual-looking stranger comes to Centerburg, causing the sheriff to be uneasy.

Chapter 6

_________ Dulcey Dooner is hired to put in much-needed street signs in the new suburb.

_________ Miss Enders lives in Centerburg and offers her property to build a new suburb.

_________ Dulcey Dooner finds the buried Cough Syrup & Elixir Compound, and the homestead is rebuilt.

_________ Uncle Ulysses is especially interested in mass producing houses and gives lots of advice.

_________ The homestead is replaced with a new suburban house, and nobody can find their own home.

_________ One hundred identical houses are built surrounding the old Enders Homestead.

Short Answer

Write a phrase or sentence for each question.

1. Describe Homer Price, the main character of this story. ______

2. How does Homer's common sense help him solve the mystery of the missing bracelet?

3. What did Miss Terwilliger do that displayed her cleverness? ______

4. What very important difference is there between Mr. Murphy and the Pied Piper at the end of the chapter?

5. Describe one benefit and one harmful effect that occurred in Centerburg as a result of mass production.

APPENDIX

Robert McCloskey (1914-2003) was born in Hamilton, Ohio. He wrote and illustrated eight books, two of which won the Caldecott Honor award, and two of which were awarded the prestigious Caldecott Medal award.

As a child growing up in a small town in the Midwest, McCloskey's parents encouraged him to pursue his interests. His love for music led him to the piano, harmonica, drums, and oboe. This love, though never abandoned, gave way later to an interest in mechanics and inventing. He tinkered with old electric trains and clocks, and even built a train with a remote control.

In high school, McCloskey's interests took another turn. He was asked to do drawings for his school annual and discovered a talent and strong love for art. This led to a college scholarship to Vesper George Art School in Boston. While in Boston, he often walked through the Public Gardens on his way to school and spent leisure time watching the ducks there. In 1934 he was given his first major art commission, and in 1936 he moved to New York City to study at the National Academy of Design and pursue a professional art career. But McCloskey had trouble selling his paintings with themes of Greek mythology and dragons, and his career never really took off. After eventually visiting a children's book editor, he was encouraged to focus on what he knew best, and in 1938 moved back to the Midwest.

In Ohio, McCloskey once again drew inspiration for his drawings from the small town setting and built up his portfolio. His first book, *Lentil*, was published in 1939; it is about the story of a boy who, when disappointed in his inability to sing, learns to play the harmonica. McCloskey was soon thereafter hired to paint murals in a wealthy Boston suburb, and moved back to the area.

In 1940, McCloskey married Peggy Durand, a children's librarian, who was the daughter of the children's author Ruth Sawyer. The McCloskeys had two children, Sally and Jane.

McCloskey's second and arguably most popular book, *Make Way for Ducklings*, was published in 1942. The story follows a mother duck searching for a suitable place in Boston to raise her young. To gain details for his drawings, he purchased six mallard ducklings, following them in his studio and watching them swim in his bathtub. The pictures came easily, but the writing was more difficult for him. He had to rewrite the book many times before he was satisfied with the end result.

Homer Price, the story of the adventures of a young inventor in the rural Midwest, followed in 1943. He continued this story later in the book *Centerburg Tales*. These books were later translated into Russian in the 1970s and became popular in the USSR.

In the late 1940s, McCloskey and his family moved to an island off the northern coast of Maine. Successive books now reflected his love of the ocean and his family. *Blueberries for Sal* featured his wife and eldest daughter, Sally. *One Morning in Maine* included his younger daughter, Jane. With the publishing of *Time of Wonder*, he became the first author to win two coveted Caldecott Medal awards. His final book, *Burt Dow: Deep-Water Man*, appeared in 1963.

Those who knew Robert McCloskey described him as a modest man concerning his skills as a writer: "It's just sort of an accident that I write books." "I really think up stories in pictures and just fill in between the pictures with a sentence or a paragraph or a few pages of words."

Rip Van Winkle

by

Washington Irving

(Adapted for younger readers by Dayna Grant)

Nestled in the foot of the Kaatskills mountains near the Hudson River, lies an idyllic village settled by Dutch colonists many years ago. In the years right before the Revolutionary War, there lived in this village a shiftless but most amiable man by the name of Rip Van Winkle. Though a husband and a father and a farmer, he worked very little at being good at any of these things. He preferred instead to work very hard at being pleasantly idle. He could be found flying kites or playing marbles with the village children who dogged his wandering steps, or telling them long stories of ghosts and witches and Indians. You might see him running an unimportant errand for a neighbor, or fishing all day without catching a single fish, or even building a neighborhood fence if it got him away from his own pressing chores at home. More often than not, you would find him lazing about on a bench in front of the village inn with his equally useless friends, gossiping or making wise pronouncements about current events. In short, Rip would happily engage in any activity except that which would be genuinely useful.

His wife was not the kind to be silent in regards to Rip's shortcomings, but her attempts to berate and nag and shame him into being a more useful sort of person failed entirely. After many years of marriage, Rip would often be forced to wander far into the woods to escape his work and his wife. One day he had wandered to the highest part of the Kaatskills mountains with his hunting rifle, and, fearing his wife's rage if he returned too late, had begun to head home when he heard someone calling his name in the distance. As he approached the voice he found a strange man in old-fashioned clothes carrying a heavy cask up the mountain. Always willing to help a neighbor, Rip helped him carry his load up the mountain to his companions.

As they approached the rest of the party, an odd sound, like the long, rolling peals of distant thunder, could be heard. They entered a hidden opening in the mountains where the man's companions, similarly dressed in outdated clothes, were playing a very serious game of bowling. All was quiet except for the echoing sound of thunder coming from the rolling ball. Rip, not one to pass up a party, no matter how strange, passed out drinks from the cask he'd helped carry up the mountain, and drank a few himself. As he drank the strange liquid, he got more and more tired until he finally fell asleep, curled on the ground.

When he awoke in the brightness of morning, his companions had vanished. The shiny hunting rifle he'd placed on the ground beside him the night before appeared to have been replaced with a rusted and rotting rifle. Confused, but knowing his wife's anger increased with every minute he failed to return home, he hurried down into the village. As he wandered through streets that seemed to have transformed overnight, he drew curious gazes and a troop of children, all of them strangely unfamiliar. He reached up to rub his chin in bewilderment, and discovered his beard had grown a foot overnight. And then he started to suspect he had slept longer than one night.

He walked to his house to find it abandoned, his wife and children absent. He walked through streets that were no longer familiar and greeted people in the streets that he didn't know. He walked to the inn to discover one of his friends had died eighteen years ago, one had died in the Revolutionary War which had taken place while he slept, and one was now a member of the Congress of the new United States of America.

Completely at a loss, Rip asked if anyone knew a man named Rip Van Winkle. "Yes!" cried the villagers. "He disappeared," they said, "some twenty years ago. He went into the woods with his hunting rifle and hasn't been seen or heard from since."

This was quite a shock to Rip, who stood before them with ragged clothes and an unruly beard, to find out that he fell asleep one night and slept for twenty years. His wife had died, they told him, and his children were all grown with children of their own.

"But I am Rip!" he cried. "Young Rip Van Winkle once—old Rip Van Winkle now! Does nobody know poor Rip Van Winkle?"

And there was much exclaiming and explaining and consulting. And finally, it was decided that he was, in fact, the very same Rip Van Winkle who had disappeared twenty years ago or yesterday, and that strange things had been known to happen deep in the Kaatskills mountains. The villagers consulted the town historian (that is to say, the oldest man in the village, who was fond of gossip and stories), and learned that Hendrick Hudson, discoverer of the Hudson River and surrounding territories, is said to return every twenty years to keep a watchful eye on his lands. The strange companions in outdated clothing Rip found bowling in the mountains must surely have been Hudson and his crew, and the contents of the cask Rip so enthusiastically drank must have bewitched him.

And while this was all rather shocking, it did not much alter the daily life of Rip Van Winkle. He soon became a favorite playmate of a new generation of children, located those of his idling friends who were still alive, and took up his spot on the bench outside the inn once more. He even became a sort of revered patriarch of the village, a relic of the time "before the war." An old man, Rip found, can be idle with impunity.

The Pied Piper of Hamelin

based on the Robert Browning poem

(Adapted for younger readers by Dayna Grant)

The charming little town of Hamelin in Brunswick, Germany, was beset nearly five hundred years ago by an infestation of rodents. Hundreds and hundreds of rats roamed the streets of Hamelin, fighting with dogs and killing cats and biting babies and ruining food. They created such a ruckus they often drowned out the sound of ladies chatting in the streets.

The townspeople, understandably, did not want these unwelcome guests in their town. The people gathered in the Town Hall and made it clear that a foolish Mayor and useless Town Councilmen who could not rid their town of rats would soon be looking for new jobs. Now, you would have to look long and hard before you found lazier or greedier men than the Mayor and the Councilmen. They very much enjoyed the usually easy and very lucrative job of running the town, so they sat down to search their empty heads for ideas.

After an hour of fruitless thinking, they gave up in despair. At that same moment, a gentle tap was heard at the chamber door, and in walked a tall, clean-shaven, colorfully attired stranger. He told the men that he was able, by means of his pipe and a secret charm, to cause any living creature to follow after him wherever he willed. The man spoke of his exploits ridding other towns of unwelcome pests and vermin, and offered to do the same for Hamelin, for a small price. The Mayor and Councilmen, giddy with relief, told the piper they'd pay him fifty times what he asked, if only he'd rid the town of rats.

The piper stepped into the street and blew three notes on his pipe. A faint rumbling began, growing louder and louder, until rats began to flow out from houses and holes. And all the rats in all the town followed the strange little piper to the river outside the town wall. One by one they all jumped in the river and drowned, except one stout rat who managed to swim across. He went back to Rat-land and told all the rats there about the man who piped three shrill notes on a pipe and made all the rats in Hamelin believe the whole world had been turned into a giant pantry. The rats of Hamelin heard the sounds of corks popping and crackers crunching and the glorious sound of cupboards opening, and they followed those sounds to the bottom of the river.

But in Hamelin, the townspeople rang bells and rejoiced and danced in the square. In the midst of this the piper's voice was heard saying, "But first, if you please, my payment!" And at this the Mayor and Town Council remembered their hasty promise of generous payment, and their greedy little hearts froze with horror. They thought of all the lovely coats and mouth-watering foods they could buy with the money they'd promised the piper and they did not want to pay him.

"You will regret this!" threatened the piper.

"Well," said they, "you've already done what we wanted. You may have a paltry payment for your services, and a drink of course, for we are not ungenerous, but then you must be on your way. For what have we to fear from you? Do your worst!"

To this pronouncement the piper gave no response. He simply stepped out into the street and blew three sweet notes on his pipe. And out of the houses and down the lanes skipped all the children of the town. They hopped and laughed and danced and happily followed the piper where he led. He guided them through the streets and past the river, and straight towards Koppelberg Hill, as the townspeople watched, helpless. And the townspeople thought, perhaps, that the piper and the children would never be able to climb over the mountain and that the children would be returned to them. But as the procession approached, a portal opened in the side of the mountain and the piper marched straight into it, the children following behind. And as the last child (excepting one little boy with a limp who couldn't keep up with the rest) ran through the portal it sealed itself up as if it had never been there.

The townspeople looked everywhere for their lost children, and the Mayor even offered a large reward to anyone who could return them, but they were never seen or heard from again. Though there is a tale, in far away Transylvania, of a strange tribe of people foreign to those lands, whose parents were said to have risen from an underground tunnel, telling remarkable stories of music and mountains and a charming little town called Hamelin.